TEACH US
TO NUMBER
OUR DAYS

STEVEN MCFADDEN is the founder and an
associate of *The Wisdom Conservancy*, an
institute dedicated to gathering the wisdom
of distinguishing elder men and women from
around the world. An author and journalist
of many years' experience, he also lectures
and travels widely.

Profiles in Wisdom

Ancient Voices, Current Affairs

*The Little Book of
  Native American Wisdom*

*Farms of Tomorrow
  (co-authored with Trauger Groh)*

TEACH US TO NUMBER OUR DAYS

Inspirational Thoughts on
Wisdom and Aging

STEVEN MCFADDEN

ELEMENT

Rockport, Massachusetts • Shaftesbury, Dorset
Brisbane, Queensland

© Steven McFadden 1996

First published in the USA in 1996 by
Element Books, Inc.
P.O. Box 830, Rockport, MA 01966

Published in Great Britain in 1996 by
Element Books Limited
Shaftesbury, Dorset SP7 8BP

Published in Australia in 1996 by
Element Books Limited for
Jacaranda Wiley Limited
33 Park Road, Milton, Brisbane 4064

Text design/composition by Paperwork
Cover by Liz Trovato
Printed and bound in the USA by Donnelley & Son Inc.

Library of Congress Cataloging in Publication
data available

British Library Cataloguing in Publication
data available

ISBN 1–85230–803–6

DEDICATION

For my grandmother,
Julia Veronica Coveney Fitzsimmons
(1895 – 1994)

PART ONE

IN LATER LIFE one sometimes has
the feeling of going into a large
church and seeing a shaft of
light coming down. That shaft
of light, perhaps, comes in the
period of life between 65 and
70. A lot of people have walked
through that shaft of light. . . .
But remember, it is the shaft
that makes the person; it isn't
the person that makes the shaft.

JOHN H. FINLEY
Personal communication

INTRODUCTION

—◆—

So teach us to number our days,
that we may apply our hearts
unto wisdom.

PSALMS 90:12

Throughout history most successful and long-lived civilizations have held a place of respect for elders, and have benefited from their life wisdom. By and large this tradition is missing today, to the detriment not only of elders but also of society.

Each moment, each day, each one of us grows older. Thanks to medical advances and wide emphasis on personal fitness, most of us will become old. The average life span has, in fact, been steadily increasing since the dawn of the twentieth century. This trend raises some critical questions: What is the purpose of a long life? What can and should older people do with their extended years? What roles do older people have in modern societies?

We might further ask: Is our civilization itself to suffer only the aches and complaints, decrepitude and debility of aging? Or, as with some human beings, could our civilization also grow old more gracefully? Could we grow in collective wisdom and its applications, attending to the elders of each generation and their concerns, while ensuring a clean, safe place for the newly born to fulfill their destinies?

Census trends show that in many Western countries, we are steadily changing from a society dominated by youths to a world populated with many more millions of older people. Rather than seeing this as a problem, as some are wont to do, we might well recognize that this also represents a great potential blessing.

One can become old simply by surviving the passage of years. But an elder is someone who has earned respect and authority by virtue of advanced age, experience, integrity, and understanding. As history shows, elders can be, and frequently have been, profoundly steadying and enriching influences both for their families and for societies.

Clearly not everyone who becomes old also becomes an elder. But some do, and many more could. In our era of raucous cultural transition, the world could gain enormously from such a development. Young people, who seem so confused about the world and their place in it, could especially benefit.

True elders are people who have gracefully accepted the passage of time, integrated their life experience with deep understanding, and made the fruit of their long experience available to others. But how does one do this? How does one become a true elder? As the title of this book echoes, the Biblical figure named Job offers a starting point that is both specific and somewhat enigmatic: *"Teach us to number our days."*

While readers may have their own understanding of what Job meant by "number our days," one apparent meaning is consciously to review and to cherish the course of one's life, to recollect what has happened. Through this deliberate process, experience may be condensed in the soul, and in various ways passed on for the benefit of generations to come.

Many memorable poems and observations about growing old and being old call to mind harsh images of sickness, senselessness, even silliness. All these conditions, it must be admitted, are very real possibilities. But they are not the only possibilities. There are other models, other realities, and deeper understandings.

Our hope is that the observations and insights gathered on the following pages will help in some small way to cleanse the windows of perception concerning other possibilities for those who are growing older – all of us – and that from this the whole of our civilization may advance.

Steven McFadden

TEACH US
TO NUMBER
OUR DAYS

THE FRUIT of old age is the memory
of abundant blessings previously
acquired.

*(Fructus autem senectutis est, ante
partorum bonorum memoria et copia.)*

MARCUS TULLIUS CICERO
De Senectute

FOR THE IGNORANT, old age is a winter;
for the learned, it is a harvest.

CHASIDIC SAYING

IT IS time to be old,
To take in sail.

RALPH WALDO EMERSON
Terminus

OLD AGE: the crown of life, our play's last act.

MARCUS TULLIUS CICERO
De Senectute

AGE IS very mysterious because the essence of
the human being – the soul – actually never
ages. It's only the outer covering of the
individual that changes.

BEATRICE WOOD
Quoted in *The Ageless Spirit*

COME, Captain Age,
With your great sea-chest full of treasure!
Under the yellow and wrinkled tarpaulin
Disclose the carved ivory
And the sandalwood inlaid with pearl:
Riches of wisdom and years.

SARAH N. CLEGHORN
Come, Captain Age

A MAN over ninety is a great comfort to all
    his elderly neighbors; he is a picket-guard
    at the extreme outpost; and the young folks
    of sixty and seventy feel that the enemy
    must get by him before he can come near
    their camp.

OLIVER WENDELL HOLMES
The Guardian Angel

AN OLD man or woman loved is
    winter with flowers.

GERMAN PROVERB

YOUTH is the time to study wisdom;
    old age is the time to practice it.

HENRI ROUSSEAU
Reveries of a Solitary Walker

OLD AGE has a great sense of calm and
freedom; when the passions relax their
hold, then . . . we are freed from the grasp
not of one mad master only, but of many.

PLATO
The Republic

. . . LOOK to the old, they are worthy of old
age; they have seen their days and proven
themselves. With the help of Great Spirit,
they have attained a ripe old age. At this
age the old can predict or give knowledge
or wisdom . . . it is so . . .

BLACK ELK
Oglala Sioux Holy Man

AGE IN a virtuous person, of either sex,
   carries in it an authority which makes it
   preferable to all the pleasures of youth.

SIR RICHARD STEELE
The Spectator

WHAT FIND YOU better or more honorable
   than age? Take the pre eminence of it in
   everything – in an old friend, in old wine,
   in an old pedigree.

SHAKERLEY MARMION
Antiquary

WITH THE ANCIENT is wisdom;
   and in length of days understanding.

JOB 12:2

OLD PLACES and old persons in their turn,
when spirit dwells in them, have an
intrinsic vitality of which youth is inca-
pable; precisely the balance and wisdom
that comes from long perspectives and
broad foundations.

GEORGE SANTAYANA
Persons and Places: My Host The World

THEN to this earthen Bowl did I adjourn
My lip the secret Well of Life to learn:
And Lip to Lip it murmur'd – 'While you live
Drink! – for once dead you never shall return.'

OMAR KHAYYÁM

HOME IS where one starts from. As we
    grow older
The world becomes stranger, the pattern
    more complicated
Of Dead and living. Not the intense moment
Isolated, with no before and after,
But a lifetime burning in every moment
And not the lifetime of one man only
But of old stones that cannot be deciphered.

T.S. ELIOT
Four Quartets

As A white candle
In a holy place,
So is the beauty
Of an aged face.

JOSEPH CAMPBELL
The Old Woman

To KNOW how to grow old is the master work
of wisdom, and one of the most difficult
chapters in the great art of living.

HENRI FREDERIC AMIEL
Journal

LET TIME that makes you homely
make you sage;

The sphere of wisdom is
the sphere of age.

THOMAS PARNELL
To an Old Beauty

IT GIVES ME great pleasure to converse with
the aged. They have been over the road
that all of us must travel, and know
where it is rough and difficult and
where it is level and easy.

PLATO
The Republic

My HEART leaps up when I behold
   A rainbow in the sky:
So it was when my life began;
So is it now I am a man;
So be it when I shall grow old
   Or let me die!
The Child is father of the Man;
And I could wish my days to be
Bound each to each by natural piety.

WILLIAM WORDSWORTH
My Heart Leaps Up When I Behold

FOR EACH AGE is a dream that is dying,
Or one that is coming to birth.

ARTHUR O'SHAUGHNESSY

OLD AGE is like a rock on which many
   founder and some find shelter.

ANONYMOUS

AGE IMPRINTS more wrinkles in the mind
   than it does on the face.

MICHEL EYQUEM DE MONTAIGNE
Essays

THIS MAN of little learning grows old like an
   ox: his flesh increases, but not his wisdom.

SUTTAPITAKA
Dhammapada

EDUCATION is the best provision for old age.

ARISTOTLE
Diogenes Laertius

WHEN I WAS a boy of 13, my father was so
ignorant I could hardly stand to have the
old man around. But when I got to be 21,
I was astonished at how much he had
learned in seven years.

MARK TWAIN
Address, 18

CRABBED AGE and youth cannot live together:
Youth is full of Pleasance, age is full of care.

WILLIAM SHAKESPEARE

YOUNG MEN think old men are fools; but old men know young men are fools.

> GEORGE CHAPMAN
> *All Fools*

ONE OF THE GOOD things about getting older is that you find you're more interesting than most of the people you meet.

> LEE MARVIN
> *The Boston Globe*

THAT SIGN of old age, extolling the past at the expense of the present.

> SYDNEY SMITH
> *Lady Holland's Memoir, Recipe for Salad*

THE BOTTOM LINE is this: By your 80s and 90s it may be too late to become a millionaire, get married or start a new career. But for most of us, it's never too late for a last shot at inner peace.

JUDY FOREMAN
columnist on aging, *The Boston Globe*

WHENEVER a man's friends begin to compliment him about looking young, he may be sure that they think he is growing old.

WASHINGTON IRVING
Bracebridge Hall

YOU JUST wake up one morning and you got it.

MOMS MABLEY

GATHER YE rosebuds while ye may
Old Time is still a-flying.

ROBERT HERRICK
To the Virgins to Make Much of Time

YOUTH is the time of getting, middle age of
improving, and old age of spending; a
negligent youth is usually attended by an
ignorant middle age, and both by an empty
old age. He that hath nothing to feed upon
but vanity and lies must needs lie down in
the bed of sorrow.

ANNE BRADSTREET
Thirty-three Meditations

TIME as he grows old teaches all things.

AESCHYLUS
Prometheus Bound

WHEN TO the sessions of sweet silent thought
I summon up remembrance of things past,
I sigh the lack of many a thing I sought,
And with old woes new wail my dear
　　times' waste.

WILLIAM SHAKESPEARE
Sonnet 30

KING DAVID and King Solomon
　　Led merry, merry lives,
With many, many lady friends
　　And many, many wives;
But when old age crept over them –
　　With many, many qualms,
King Solomon wrote the Proverbs,
　　And King David wrote the Psalms.

JAMES BALL NAYLOR
Ancient Authors

I SPEAK TRUTH, not so much as I would,
   but as much as I dare; and I dare a
   little more, as I grow older.

MICHEL EYQUEM DE MONTAIGNE
Essays

ALL EXPERIENCE is an arch to build upon.

HENRY BROOKS ADAMS
The Education of Henry Adams

SO PEACEFUL shalt thou end thy blissful days
And steal thyself from life by slow decays.

HOMER
The Odyssey

AGE is opportunity no less
Than youth itself, though in another dress,
And as the evening twilight fades away
The sky is filled with stars, invisible by day.

HENRY WADSWORTH LONGFELLOW
Morituri Salutamus

OLD AGE has a great sense of calm and
freedom; when the passions relax their
hold, then . . . we are freed from the grasp
not of one mad master only, but of many.

PLATO
The Republic

GOD GIVES US LOVE. Something to love
He lends us; but when love is grown
To ripeness, that on which it throve
Falls off, and love is left alone.

ALFRED LORD TENNYSON
To J.S. (1842)

CAST ME NOT OFF in the time of old age;
forsake me not when my strength faileth.

PSALMS 71:9

PEOPLE will not look forward to posterity who
never look backward to their ancestors.

EDMUND BURKE
Reflections on the Revolutions in France

YOUNG MEN'S minds are always changeable,
but when an old man is concerned in a
matter, he looks both before and after.

HOMER
The Iliad

IN OLD AGE wandering on a trail of beauty
lively may I walk.

In old age wandering on a trail of beauty
living again may I walk.

It is finished in beauty.

NAVAJO NIGHTWAY CHANT

THE YOUNG MAN who has not wept
is a savage, and the old man who
will not laugh is a fool.

GEORGE SANTAYANA
Dialogues in Limbo

. . . (WHEN YOU ARE OLD) you have a lot of experience you can call upon, you have a kind of wisdom that leaves out the details and simply goes straight for the important things. This is the meaning of the wisdom of the ages.

ROLLO MAY
Quoted in *The Ageless Spirit*

THE ACCUMULATED experience of elders offers the context and wherewithal for the enthusiasm of youngsters. If youngsters see that old age is a barren time of isolation and illness, they will lack enthusiasm for life.

ANDREW ROTHOVIUS
The Wisdom Conservancy Advisory Council

THE ISOLATION of old people in this country
and the segregation of old people is deadly,
deadly. We old folks need to be the mentors
of the young. The young need us just as
much as we need them.

MAGGIE KUHN
The Gray Panthers

HERE ARE the proper occupations of old age:
prayer, which is the quickening of the
mind, the rooting of the attention in the
ground of being; song, which is the ex-
pression of spontaneous joy in the harmony
of the chaos; the telling of old tales, which
among all primitives was the supreme
function of the old, who passed on the
wisdom . . .

HELEN LUKE
Old Age: Journey into Simplicity

TEACH ME to live, that I may dread
The grave as little as my bed.

BISHOP THOMAS KEN
Morning and Evening Hymn

MAY I GOVERN my passions with
    absolute sway,
And grow older and wiser and better,
    as strength wears away,
Without gout or stone, by a gentle decay.

WALTER POPE
The Old Man's Wish

HE WHO is of a calm and happy nature will
    hardly feel the pressure of age, but to him
    who is of an opposite disposition, youth
    and age are equally a burden.

PLATO
The Republic

THOUGH I LOOK OLD, yet I am strong
    and lusty,
For in my youth I never did apply
Hot and rebellious liquors in my blood;
Nor did not with unbashful forehead woo
The means of weakness and debility;
Therefore my age is as a lusty winter,
Frosty, but kindly.

WILLIAM SHAKESPEARE
As You Like It

THUS FARES it still in our decay:
And yet the wiser mind
Mourns less for what age takes away
Than what it leaves behind.

WILLIAM WORDSWORTH
The Fountain

TO BE SEVENTY years young is sometimes
far more cheerful and hopeful than to be
forty years old.

OLIVER WENDELL HOLMES
Letter to Julia Ward Howe
on her seventieth birthday

AN AGE that melts with unperceived
decay,
And glides in modest innocence away;
Whose peaceful day Benevolence endears,
Whose night congratulating Conscience
cheers;
The general favorite as the general friend:
Such age there is, and who shall wish
its end?

SAMUEL JOHNSON
Vanity of Human Wishes

YET TIME, who changes all, had altered him
In soul and aspect as in age:
Years steal fire from the mind as vigor
    from the limb;
And life's enchanted cup but sparkles
    near the brim.

LORD BYRON
Childe Harold

THE TREE of deepest root is found
Least willing still to quit the ground:
'Twas therefore said by ancient sages,
That love of life increased with years
So much, that in our latter stages,
When pain grows sharp, and sickness rages,
The greatest love of life appears.

HESTER L. PIOZZI
Three Warnings

NOT ONE of them who took up in his youth
with this opinion that there are no gods
ever continued until old age faithful to
his conviction.

PLATO
Laws

AND ALMOST everyone when age,
Disease, or sorrows strike him,
Inclines to think there is a God,
Or something very like Him.

ARTHUR HUGH CLOUGH
Dipsychus

OLD AGE, especially when crowned with honor,
enjoys an authority which is of more value
than all the sensual pleasures of youth.

MARCUS TULLIUS CICERO
De Senectute

FATHER TIME is not always a hard parent, and, though he tarries for none of his children, often lays his hand lightly on those who have used him well.

> CHARLES DICKENS
> *Barnaby Rudge*

TIME HAS laid his hand upon my heart gently, not smiting it; but as a harper lays his open palm upon his harp, to deaden its vibrations.

> HENRY WADSWORTH LONGFELLOW
> *The Golden Legend Part IV, The Cloisters*

GRANT ME, sound of body and of mind, to pass an old age lacking neither honor nor the lyre.

> HORACE
> *Odes*

GROW OLD along with me!
The best is yet to be,
The last of life, for which the first was made.

ROBERT BROWNING
Rabbi Ben Ezra

OLD PEOPLE like to give good advice, as
solace for no longer being able to provide
bad examples.

FRANÇOIS, DUC DE LA ROCHEFOUCAULD
Reflections

TEARS, idle tears, I know not what they mean,
Tears from the depth of some divine despair
Rise in the heart, and gather to the eyes,
In looking on the happy autumn fields,
And thinking of the days that are no more.

ALFRED LORD TENNYSON
Tears, Idle Tears

LIFE IS A COUNTRY that the old have seen, and
lived in. Those who have to travel through
it can only learn the way from them.

JOSEPH JOUBERT
Pensées

DARLING, I am growing old,
Silver threads among the gold
Shine upon my brow today;
Life is fading fast away.

EBEN EUGENE REXFORD
Silver Threads Among the Gold

FEW PEOPLE know how to be old.

FRANÇOIS, DUC DE LA ROCHEFOUCAULD
Reflections

WORK FOR this life as though you are
    going to live forever.
Work for the Next life as though you will
    die tomorrow.

'ALI IBN ABU TALIB

No FALSEHOOD lingers into old age.

SOPHOCLES
Acrisius

I HAVE seen the moment of my greatness flicker,
And I have seen the eternal Footman hold
my coat and snicker,
And in short, I was afraid.

T.S. ELIOT
The Love Song of J. Alfred Prufrock

GRAY HAIRS seem to my fancy like the
light of a soft moon, silvering over the
evening of life.

JEAN PAUL RICHTER
Critical and Miscellaneous Essays

LIFE GROWS darker as we go on, till only one
pure light is left shining on it; and that is
faith. Old age, like solitude and sorrow, has
its revelations.

MADAME SWETCHINE

GODS ALONE have neither age nor death!
   All other things almighty Time disquiets.

SOPHOCLES
Oedipus at Colonus

NO ONE IS SO OLD that he cannot live
   yet another year, nor so young that
   he cannot die today.

FERNANDO DE ROJAS
La Celestina

LIVING IS NOT THE GOAL, but living well.
   The wise man therefore lives as long as
   he should, not as long as he can.

SENECA
Epistles

A LITTLE MORE tired at close of day,
A little less anxious to have our way;
A little less ready to scold and blame;
A little more care of a brother's name;
And so we are nearing the journey's end,
Where time and eternity meet and blend.

ROLLIN J. WELLS
Growing Old

A BLESSED DEATH comes only to those who
have lived long enough to understand
the meaning of their own story.

SOPHOCLES
Ajax

As we grow old . . . the beauty steals inward.

> Ralph Waldo Emerson
> *Journals, 1845*

When a noble life has prepared old age,
it is not the decline that it reveals, but
the first days of immortality.

> Madame de Staël

It is our task in our time and in our
generation to hand down undiminished to
those who come after us, as was handed
down to us by those who went before, the
natural wealth and beauty which is ours.

> John F. Kennedy
> March 3, 1961

PART TWO

WISDOM is like electricity. There
is no permanently wise man,
but men capable of wisdom,
who, being put into certain
company, or other favorable
conditions, become wise for a
short time, as glasses rubbed
acquire electric power for a
time.

RALPH WALDO EMERSON
Society and Solitude

INTRODUCTION

> So teach us to number our days
> THAT WE MAY APPLY OUR HEARTS
> UNTO WISDOM.
>
> PSALMS 90:12

WHAT DOES it mean to be wise? What are wise people like, and how did they gain their wisdom? What would the world look like if it were populated with thousands upon thousands of wise elders who had earned, and were benefiting from, the respect of the rest of the people? In the matter of wisdom, what are the touchstones? Around what points might we orient our strivings?

These are some of the questions that led *The Wisdom Conservancy* to gather the observations of great writers and thinkers, and to compile them in an easily accessible form.

As defined in common works of reference, wisdom is the faculty of judging rightly in matters relating to life and conduct, the ability to see truly what is right and fitting, and the capacity to act accordingly. Wisdom apparently has little to do with book learning, and is not necessarily correlated with age.

Wisdom is a manner or style of being – a knowing. One widely held understanding of wisdom is that it brings results not necessarily in harmony with human will or intention, but rather in harmony with Divine Will.

Over the millennia, millions upon millions of women and men in every culture have grown old. Many thousands have also grown wise, while some few hundred have been regarded as sages – people who are profoundly wise.

As problems mount in the modern world, our times impose a responsibility upon us: a moral obligation to come to grips with the necessity for wisdom in our individual and collective lives. Growing crises in the environment, the family, and the workplace challenge all – each and every one who can recognize what is happening – to reach toward wisdom: to rise to his or her highest, noblest, and most knowledgeable.

The Wisdom Conservancy takes it as an article of faith that this goal is neither abstract nor illusory, but that wisdom is attainable for most if not all human beings. Wisdom, we believe, is democratic, accessible to all. Most people, however, never deliberately attempt to find it, never strive consciously in this direction. Many of those who do so, with discipline, succeed.

About this quest, we offer one caveat: all the fine ideas and words in the world do not make one wise. Ultimately, wisdom is about who you are and how you live your life.

Our sincere wish is that the observations on the following pages will support you, the reader, as you strive *"to apply your heart to wisdom."*

STEVEN MCFADDEN

THAT WE
MAY APPLY
OUR HEARTS
UNTO
WISDOM

THE ONLY WISDOM we can hope to acquire
Is the wisdom of humility: humility is
endless.

RALPH WALDO EMERSON
Society and Solitude

THE BEGINNING of wisdom is
the definition of terms.

SOCRATES
Apology

WISDOM is the knowledge of things human
and divine and of the causes by which
those things are controlled.

MARCUS TULLIUS CICERO
De Officiis

WISDOM is a stream put forth from the
Great Mystery, beyond concepts, words,
or form.

DHYANI YWAHOO
Voices of Our Ancestors

IN THE CONFUCIAN sense, to know that what
is best for me is not necessarily best for my
neighbor is the beginning of wisdom . . .

TU WEI-MING
A World of Ideas II

WISDOM is divided into two parts: (a) having a
great deal to say, and (b) not saying it.

ANONYMOUS

WISDOM is to the soul what health is
to the body.

FRANÇOIS, DUC DE LA ROCHEFOUCAULD
Maximes Posthumes

THE INVARIABLE mark of wisdom is to see
the miraculous in the common.

RALPH WALDO EMERSON
Essays, Experience

THIS IS THE MARK of men just and wise as well
– even in calamity not to cherish anger
against the gods.

AESCHYLUS
Fragments

THE WISE do not grieve for the things they
have not, but rejoice for that which
they have.

EPICETUS
Fragments

A WISE MAN hears one word and
understands two.

YIDDISH PROVERB

COMMON SENSE in an uncommon degree is
what the world calls wisdom.

SAMUEL TAYLOR COLERIDGE
Table Talk

WISDOM is the accumulation of deep understanding about our experiences of being
human: knowledge about the mind, its
capacities and delusions, the pains and
strengths of the body, and the joys and
sufferings of the heart.

JUDE ROZHON
Personal communiation

WISDOM does not belong to one person.
We need to act in accord with wisdom,
but it does not belong to anyone. It is the
illumination of old and proven ideas
through generation after generation of
discovering natural law.

HUNBATZ MEN, MAYAN ELDER
Quoted in *Profiles in Wisdom*

WISDOM and goodness are twin-born,
one heart
Must hold both sisters, never seen apart.

EDMUND BURKE
Expostulations

O WORLD, thou choosest not the better part!
It is not wisdom to be only wise,
And on the inward vision close the eyes,
But it is wisdom to believe the heart.

GEORGE SANTAYANA
O World, Thou Choosest Not

THE HEART of the wise ones lies quiet
　 like limpid water.

CAMEROON PROVERB

THE TONGUE of the wise lieth
　 behind the heart.

ALI IBN-ABI-TALIB
Sentences

GREAT WISDOM is generous; petty wisdom
is contentious.

CHUANG TZU
On Leveling All Things

WISDOM excelleth folly, as far as light
excelleth darkness.

ECCLESIASTES 2:13

IT IS THE WISDOM of the crocodiles, that
shed tears when they would devour.

FRANCIS BACON

AFTER THE event even a fool is wise.

HOMER
Illiad

WISDOM is ofttimes nearer when we stoop
Than when we soar.

WILLIAM WORDSWORTH
The Excursion

THE CLOUDS may drop down titles and
estates;
Wealth may seek us; but wisdom must
be sought.

EDWARD YOUNG
Night Thoughts

HE THAT has grown to wisdom hurries not,
But thinks and weighs what wisdom
bids him do.

GUINICELLI
Of Moderation and Tolerance

60

THE MARK of wisdom is to read aright the
present, and to march with the occasion.

HOMER
Contest of Hesiod and Homer

TRUE WISDOM consists not only in seeing
what is before your eyes, but in foreseeing
what is to come.

TERENCE
Adelphi I

WISDOM does not show itself so much in
precept as in life – in a firmness of mind
and a mastery of appetite. It teaches us to
do, as well as to talk; and to make our
words and actions all of a color.

SENECA
Epistulae Mores

THE MOST certain sign of wisdom is a
continual cheerfulness; her state is like
that of things in the regions above the
moon, always clear and serene.

MICHEL EYQUEM DE MONTAIGNE
Essays I

UNLESS YOU GROW wise of yourself, you will
listen in vain to the wise.

PUBLIUS SYRUS
Sententiae

BOW DOWN thine ear, and hear the words
of the wise, and apply thine heart unto
my knowledge.

PROVERBS 22:7

ONE WISE MAN'S verdict outweighs
all the fools'.

ROBERT BROWNING
Bishop Blougram's Apology

IN THE MORNING the ignorant man considers
what he will do, while the intelligent man
considers what it is Allah will do with him.

IBN 'ATA'ILLAH

IF YOU WISH to live wisely, ignore sayings –
including this one.

HEYWOOD BROUN
It Seems to Me

WHERE THERE IS CHARITY and wisdom,
    there is neither fear nor ignorance.

Where there is patience and humility,
    there is neither anger nor vexation.

Where there is poverty and joy,
    there is neither greed nor avarice.

Where there is peace and meditation,
there is neither anxiety nor doubt.

ST. FRANCIS OF ASSISI
Counsels of the Holy Father

AS IS THE GARDEN such is the gardener.

HEBREW SAYING

WITH THE ANCIENT is wisdom; and in
    length of days understanding.

> JOB 12:2

FROM THE ERRORS of others a wise man
    corrects his own.

> PUBLIUS SYRUS
> *Moral Sayings*

WHEN THE HIGHEST type of men hear Tao,
    They diligently practice it.
When the average type of men hear Tao,
    They half believe in it.
When the lowest type of men hear Tao,
    They laugh heartily at it.

> LAO TZU
> *The Way of Lao Tzu*

Wisdom and goodness to the vile seem vile . . .

William Shakespeare
King Lear

Miss not the discourse of the elders.

Wisdom of Sirach 8:9

Wisdom is meaningless until our own
experience has given it meaning.

Bergen Evans
The Spoor of Spooks, and Other Nonsense

He who learns the rules of wisdom,
without conforming to them in his life,
is like a man who labored in his fields,
but did not sow.

Saadi

A MAN should never be ashamed to own
    he has been in the wrong, which is but
    saying, in other words, that he is wiser
    today than he was yesterday.

ALEXANDER POPE
Thoughts on Various Subjects

WISDOM comes through suffering.

AESCHYLUS
Agamemnon

WISDOM has taught us to be calm and meek,
To take one blow, and turn the other cheek;
It is not written what a man shall do
If the rude caitiff smite the other too!

OLIVER WENDELL HOLMES

TROUBLE brings experience, and experience
brings wisdom.

YIDDISH PROVERB

THE LIFE which is unexamined is not
worth living.

PLATO
Apology

FULL WYS is he that kan hymselven knowe.

GEOFFREY CHAUCER
Canterbury Tales, The Monk's Tale

KNOW THYSELF

INSCRIPTION, Temple of Delphi

HE WHO KNOWS others is wise;
He who knows himself is enlightened.

> LAO TZU
> *The Way of Lao Tzu*

THE ART of being wise is the art of
knowing what to overlook.

> WILLIAM JAMES
> *The Principles of Psychology*

LOGICAL consequences are the scarecrows
of fools and the beacons of wise men.

> THOMAS HENRY HUXLEY
> *Animal Automatism*

THE WISE know too well their weaknesses
to assume infallibility.

THOMAS JEFFERSON
Writings

KNOWLEDGE is proud that he has learn'd
so much;
Wisdom is humble that he knows
no more.

WILLIAM COWPER
Epistle to Joseph Hill

IT IS EASIER to be wise for others than
for ourselves.

FRANÇOIS, DUC DE LA ROCHEFOUCAULD
Maximes

THE FIRST STEP toward madness is
to think oneself wise.

FERNANDO DE ROJAS
La Celestina

ASK, who is wise? – you'll find the
self-same man

A sage in France, a madman in Japan.

THOMAS MOORE
The Sceptic

WISE MEN profit more from fools than fools
from wise men; for the wise men shun the
mistakes of fools, but the fools do not
imitate the successes of the wise.

PLUTARCH
Lives (Marcus Porcius Cato, the Elder)

IT TAKES a wise man to recognize a wise man.

XENOPHANES
Diogenes Laertius

THE SAGE does not accumulate for himself.
The more he gives to others,
    the more he possesses of his own.
The more he uses for others,
    the more he has himself.
The more he gives to others,
    the more he possesses of his own.
The Way of Heaven is to benefit others,
    and not to injure.
The way of the sage is to act,
    but not compete.

LAO TZU
The Way of Lao Tzu

WISDOM consists in rising superior both to
    madness and to common sense, and in
    lending one's self to the universal delusion
    without becoming its dupe.

AMIEL (MRS. HUMPHREY WARD)
Journal, December 11, 1872

FOR IN HER [wisdom] is a spirit intelligent,
    holy, unique, manifold, subtle, agile, clear,
    unstained, certain, not baneful, loving the
    good, keen, unhampered, beneficent,
    kindly, firm, secure, tranquil, all-powerful,
    all-seeing, and pervading all spirits, though
    they be intelligent, pure and very subtle.

WISDOM OF SOLOMON 7:22–23

IT IS characteristic of wisdom not to do
desperate things.

HENRY DAVID THOREAU
Walden

TO BE A philosopher is not merely to have
subtle thoughts, nor even to found a school,
but so to love wisdom as to live accordingly
to its dictates, a life of simplicity, indepen-
dence, magnanimity, and trust.

HENRY DAVID THOREAU
Walden

KNOWLEDGE comes, but wisdom lingers.

ALFRED LORD TENNYSON

WISDOM is not finally tested in the schools,

Wisdom cannot be pass'd from one having
   it to another not having it,

Wisdom is of the Soul, is not susceptible of
   proof, is its own proof.

WALT WHITMAN
Song of the Open Road

THERE IS no happiness where there is no
   wisdom, no wisdom but in submission
   to the gods. Big words are always punished,
   and proud men in old age learn to be wise.

SOPHOCLES
Antigone

WHERE ignorance is bliss, 'tis folly to be wise.

THOMAS GRAY
On a Distant Prospect of Eton College

To FLEE VICE is the beginning of virtue,
  and to have got rid of folly is
  the beginning of wisdom.

HORACE
Epistles

THIS WAS EVER the world's distempered will:

Fools have always mocked and spurned
    the wise.

These shall be judged according to their lies.

WALTHER VON DER VOGELWEIDE
Lament

NOT BY AGE but by capacity is
wisdom acquired.

TITUS MACCIUS PLAUTUS
Trinummus

NO ONE was ever wise by chance.

SENECA
Epistulae ad Lucilium

IN SEEKING WISDOM, thou art wise;
in imaging that thou hast attained it,
thou art a fool.

RABBI BEN-AZAI

AUTHORITY without wisdom is like
   a heavy ax without an edge, fitter
   to bruise than polish.

ANNE BRADSTREET
Thirty-three Meditations

TO KNOW

That which before us lies in daily life
Is the prime wisdom.

JOHN MILTON
Paradise Lost

HE WHO HAS begun is half done.
   Dare to be wise; begin!

HORACE
Epistles

UNTIL PHILOSOPHERS are kings, or the kings
and princes of this world have the spirit and
power of philosophy, and political greatness
and wisdom meet in one, and those
commoner natures who pursue either to
the exclusion of the other are compelled
to stand aside, cities will never have rest
from their evils.

PLATO
The Republic

IT IS SAID that an Eastern monarch once
charged his wise men to invent him a
sentence to be ever in view, and which
should be true and appropriate in all times
and situations. They presented him the
words: "And this, too, shall pass away."

ABRAHAM LINCOLN,
Address, September 30, 1859

RESPLENDENT and unfading is Wisdom, and
she is readily perceived by those who love
her, and found by those who seek her.

WISDOM OF SOLOMON 6:12

BE WISELY worldly, not worldly wise.

FRANCIS QUARLES
Divine Fancies

WISDOM is the principal thing; therefore
get wisdom: and with all thy getting
get understanding.

PROVERBS 4:7

DEFER NOT till tomorrow to be wise,
Tomorrow's sun to thee may never rise.

WILLIAM CONGREVE
Letter to Cobham

ONLY THROUGH the rhythmic swing of the
pendulum between Wisdom and Love, not
through sleepy rest, will the future be
rightly formed.

RUDOLF STEINER
Quoted by Richard Seddon in
The End of the Millennium

NOBODY grows old merely by
living a number of years. People
grow old by deserting their
ideals. Years wrinkle the skin,
but to give up interest wrinkles
the soul.

ZOROASTER
advising Cyrus the Great

ACKNOWLEDGMENTS

THE COMPILER and the publisher acknowledge and offer thanks to all the women and men whose words, in synthesis, constitute this volume. Every effort has been made to cite accurately the author and the work from which their words are drawn. Some authors and publishers have requested specific wording for acknowledgment, and those requests are honored below.

The quotation on page 15 is drawn from "East Coker, " part of *Four Quartets*, (*Collected Poems 1909–1962* by T. S. Eliot), published by Harcourt Brace & Jovanovich in the US; Faber and Faber, Ltd –World Rights.

Index of Authors

THE WISDOM CONSERVANCY
at Merriam Hill Education Center

148 Merriam Hill

Greenville, NH 03048

USA